Wonderfully Made

For my sweet girl, Haven

God designed you exactly the way you are for an exact purpose. Your worth in the Lord is so much more than what this world may say about you.

I want you to always remember how intelligent, kind, loving, funny, sweet, beautiful, and godly you are.

God has called you to a higher purpose, and I pray daily that you will always look in the mirror and see yourself through God's loving eyes.

I adore you more than you'll ever know.

XOXO Mom

Little *Haven* was getting dressed one morning to go to church, but she couldn't decide what to wear.

She tried on all she had with nothing left to spare.

Haven tried on a purple dress, a blue dress, a green dress, an orange dress, a red dress, and a pink dress!

She looked in the mirror and still felt like a mess!

Haven sat at the mirror and tears started to fall.

She wondered why she didn't feel pretty at all.

In the corner of her eye,
she saw a cross on the wall.

That's when *Haven* remembered
the book that holds the answers to all.

Haven stood up from the floor and opened the drawer.

She found her pink Bible patiently waiting to be explored.

Haven opened her Bible, and found a surprise!

As she kept reading, she couldn't believe her eyes!

The page she opened to was in the book of Psalms.

As little *Haven* kept reading, she suddenly felt calm.

She looked in the mirror, and smiled with both hands raised.

"I will praise you," little *Haven* proclaimed. "For I am fearfully and wonderfully made!"

Haven started twirling in her pretty, pink dress.

She smiled, remembering God's ways are truly the best.

Everyone is different,
that's how we were designed!

God's hand has been on us
since the beginning of time . . .

. . . from the color of our eyes, to the freckles on our skin, to the length of our hair, to the shape of our chin!

We each have different qualities and that's okay!

God wouldn't want to have it any other way!

The next time *Haven* is sad, she'll know where to turn!

She'll open up her Bible and continue to learn!

Author Lacey Ens

Lacey Ens grew up in New Brunswick, Canada, and currently lives in British Columbia with her husband and their two beautiful children.

She loves being a stay-at-home mom and finds joy in photography, embroidery, pretty fields, yummy iced coffees, and spending time with God's people.

Hi, I'm Lacey Ens! I have always dreamed of writing a faith-based book for kids.
After having children of my own, I see the need for more faith-based children's books.
I'm so excited to share my first book "Wonderfully Made" with you!

Please join my newsletter mailing list. I'd love to hear from you!

book.wonderfullymade@gmail.com | https://bookwonderfullymade.wixsite.com

Artist Megan Lane

Megan Lane was born and raised in Nova Scotia, Canada.

She resides in a cozy home with her husband, John, and their miniature schnauzer, Maudie.

She has a passion for creating images that celebrate the beauty of simple homes, rural landscapes, and the natural world.

Through her work, Megan seeks to evoke feelings of nostalgia, belonging, and a comforting sense of home.

View her art on Instagram @meganlanedraws

Thank You

First, I want to thank my amazing husband, Caleb. You have stood by my side and supported this writing dream of mine no matter our circumstances. Thank you for always encouraging me, loving me, and supporting me. I love and appreciate you dearly.

Secondly, my parents, Paula and Jeff Munn. You have contributed a lot to help make my book come to life. You have always loved me and believed that I could achieve anything since I was a little girl. I am so thankful and I have so much love for you both.

Ashley Carpenter and Michelle Fowler, your kindness and friendships mean a lot to me. Thank you for helping me make this happen.

I couldn't have accomplished this book without each of you. Thank you from the bottom of my heart.

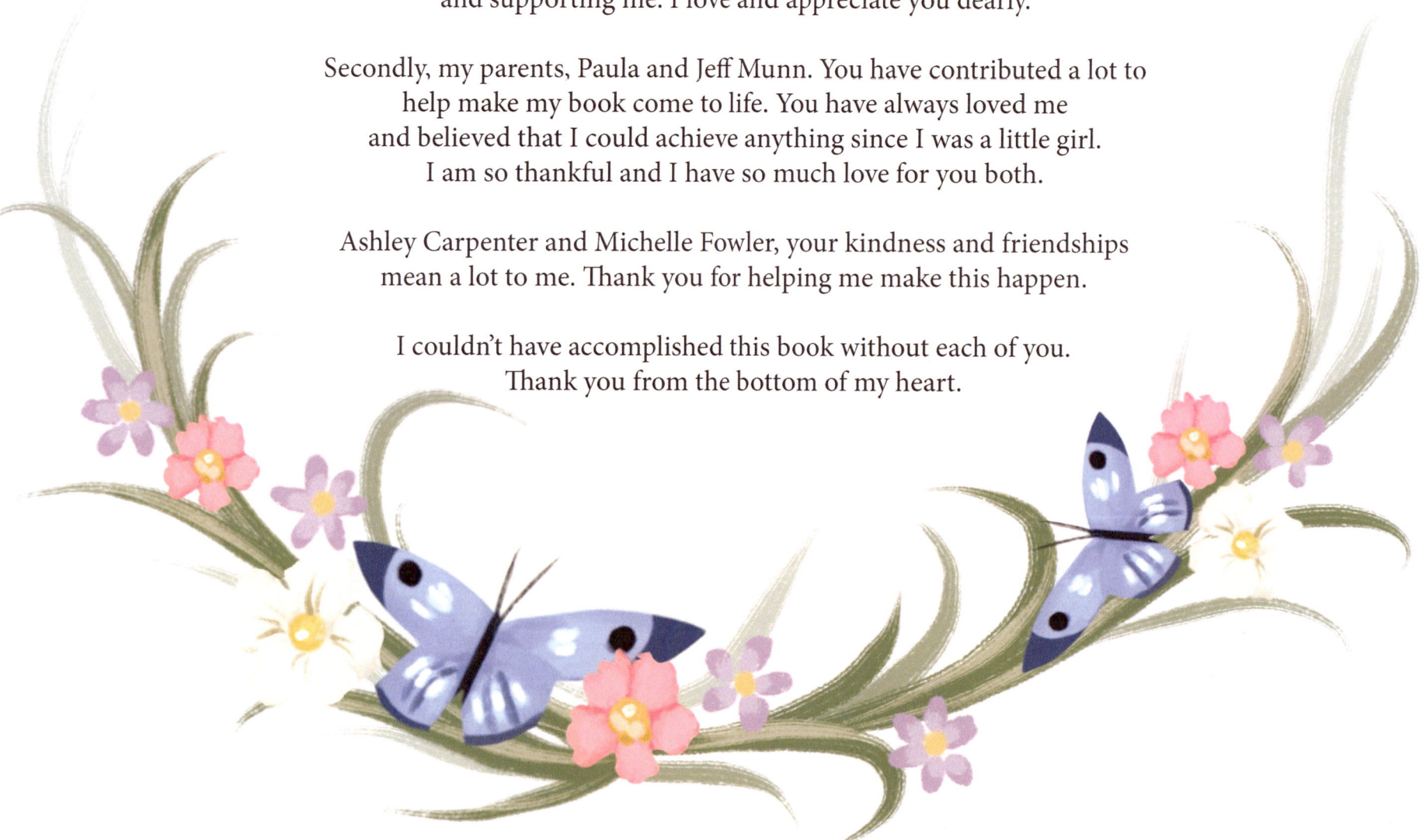

www.ingramcontent.com/pod-product-compliance
Lightning Source LLC
Chambersburg PA
CBRC101522070526
44586CB00010B/94